A Room with a View
by E. M. Forster

A Study Guide by R.A. Moore

Picture: Portrait of E. M. Forster (1924 or 1925) by Dora Carrington (1893–1932). A public domain image from Wikimedia Commons.

Use of the text of *A Room With a View*: The copyright on this text has expired and it is therefore in the public domain.

Acknowledgements:
To all my students through the years who taught me so much about this book. Special thanks to my wife Barbara for preparing the text for publication

Contents

A Room with a View by E. M. Forster

Dramatis personae (List of Characters)

The Honeychurch family:
Lucy Honeychurch - The protagonist of the novel. She doesn't know what she wants. She struggles between choosing love or following the dictates of society.
Mr. Honeychurch - Lucy's late father who was a prosperous builder.
Mrs. Honeychurch - Lucy's widowed mother. She is a good mother, not cultured or sophisticated, but she understands people. Unfortunately, she is a snob.
Freddy Honeychurch - Lucy's nineteen year-old brother. He is devoted to his sister, dislikes her fiancé Cecil, but likes George. He appears to be a rebel, but a lot of it is just show.
Charlotte Bartlett - A prim old spinster. Lucy's older cousin and chaperone in Italy. There is, however, a secret in her past.

The Emerson Family:
Mr. Emerson - George's widowed lower-middle class father. A retired journalist who is completely unaware of the limits of society's conventions.
George Emerson - Of a lower social class than Lucy he has a clerical job with a railway company.

The Vyse Family:
Mrs. Vyse - Cecil's upper-middle class mother, who is a widow living in London. She is a woman of culture and refinement but lacking in spirit and vitality
Cecil Vyse - Lucy's fiancé, a well educated young man who likes London society
Italian driver and his girlfriend - They are what Lucy and George should be.

People we meet in Italy:
The Reverend Arthur Beebe - He will become he minister of Lucy's church in her home village of Summer Street.
Minnie Beebe - The minister's niece who frequently stays as a guest of the Honeychurches.
Miss Eleanor Lavish - A shocking lady novelist (a.k.a. Joseph Emery Prank).
The Miss Alans - Two elderly spinster sisters, Theresa and Catherine who stay at the same pension in Florence as Lucy and later invite her to travel to Greece with them.
Mr. Eager - The British chaplain in Florence, who perpetuates a false rumor that Mr. Emerson murdered his wife.

People we meet in England:
Sir Harry Otway - The local squire in Summer Street who buys two villas and leases one of them to the Emersons. He enjoys his high social position, but Cecil finds him vulgar.

Themes

Head versus Heart:

Are you a person who is ruled by your Head (the intellect, rationality, logic, reason) or by your Heart (the emotions, feelings, instincts, passions)? Chances are that it is a little of both, although you probably acknowledge one to be a stronger influence than the other.

E. M. Forster feels that the English are ruled almost exclusively by their Heads - particularly the English middle and upper classes into which he was born. The 'cold-blooded' Englishman and the English 'stiff upper lip' are manifestations of this rationality. As a result, these people do not really *live*; they suppress their desires, control their urges, and finally kill the vital spark of life itself. In contrast, Forster presents the Italians as not having cultivated rationality. As a result they are ruled by their Hearts: they act on impulse, and fall into hatred as quickly as they fall into love. If the English are adults, then the Italians are children, and the results are disastrous for each. The solution, Forster believes, is to *connect* the Head and the Heart: to live in balance, to live as Nature intends man to live. In doing this, Mr. Emerson says, men will enter the Garden of Eden, which is not a lost paradise but an end we have yet to attain.

Adults, Children and Muddle:

Even the English are influenced by their Hearts when they are children, but the adults soon put an end to that. Children are taught their manners: to act politely, to dress properly, to speak nicely, to follow the rules of etiquette, etc. By the time they are 18 years old, they are young ladies and gentlemen, cookie-cutter versions of their rational parents. It is all very sad.

'Muddle' occurs when a young person wants to follow his/her heart but instead does or says what the adults would want, or expect, or demand that he/she do. The result is that the young person is actually a traitor to his/her own Heart, parroting the 'wisdom' of adults.

Delicacy versus Beauty:

English middle class society had its rules of etiquette and decorum governing all aspect of social behavior. Whole books were written to explain the rules of behaving delicately, that is, never giving offence to anyone. (Even our society today has these rules, which is why you say you are going to the 'restroom' or the 'bathroom' instead of telling everyone in the room that you are going to the 'toilet'.)

Beautiful actions are based upon impulses of feeling uncensored by considerations of propriety: opening a conversation with a lady to whom you have not been introduced; giving a lady you do not know very well a bunch of flowers; advising someone on their health in public at the dinner table. (All of these actually happen in the novel.)

A Room with a View by E. M. Forster

The American writer Henry Miller put it brilliantly, "Every day we slaughter our finest impulses. That is why we get a heartache when we read those lines written by the hand of a master and recognize them as our own, as the tender shoots which we stifled because we lacked the faith to believe in our own powers, our own criterion of truth and beauty. Every man, when he gets quiet, when he becomes desperately honest with himself, is capable of uttering profound truths. We all derive from the same source. There is no mystery about the origin of things. We are all part of creation, all kings, all poets, all musicians; we have only to open up, only to discover what is already there." (*Sexus*)

Social Class:

In Edwardian England, the social class into which one was born pretty much determined the life one would lead; social mobility was small. One married within one's class to a person who was socially acceptable. Attractive young women, from good families, might often marry 'up', that is, marry men from slightly better families and/or families with more money. (If you have read Jane Austen's *Pride and Prejudice*, you will know all about that. Here's the first line, "It is a truth universally acknowledged, that a single man in possession of a good fortune, must be in want of a wife.") However, for a woman to marry 'down', that is, below her own class was almost unheard of. Marriage was often more a financial contract than a romantic, loving union.

The biggest social gap in English society was between those who worked for a living (the working and lower-middle classes) and those who had independent mean which they had inherited and which brought in an income from investments (the upper-middle class and above). There was a great deal of snobbery about 'old money' being superior to 'new money', even when the person with 'new money' was actually richer! (If you have read Scott Fitzgerald's *The Great Gatsby*, you will know all about that.)

Romantic Love and Physical Love:

In an age when both women and men covered as much flesh with their clothes as was possible, the whole topic of sex was off the table. Of course, married people (and *only* married people) did have sex, but that was just to have children; no one (particularly no lady) actually enjoyed it; it was a wife's 'duty'. This being so, two young people could not admit, either to themselves or to each other, that they were sexually attracted to each other. If they spoke of being in love at all, they spoke in terms of an idealized, romantic love such as poets write about.

Forster believed that there was no distinction between being romantically in love and being physically attracted. "Love is of the body," says Mr. Emerson. To deny the physical in balance with the emotional is to deny man's true nature.

When Forster writes about the 'forbidden love' of Lucy and George and how it finally triumphs over the external and internal barriers erected to prevent it, he also has another social taboo in mind. Forster was homosexual at a time when homosexuality was a crime for which one could be tried and put in jail. (Recall the famous case of writer Oscar Wilde.) In describing how Lucy and George come to understand that they are in love body and soul (Heart and Head), he is also writing about the right of gay people to the same loving relationships which his society only allowed heterosexuals. Only in one novel did Forster actually deal openly with homosexual love, *Maurice* which was published in 1971 after his death.

Literary devices in the novel

Setting:
The first half of the novel is set in Italy and the Second half in England in the first decade of the twentieth century. The English people who have travelled to Italy actually recreate England in Florence (their hotel might as well be in London; they attend their Protestant church not the local Catholic churches; they take guided tours to learn the history of Italy whilst avoiding its present, etc.); the last thing they actually want to do is to explore the 'real Italy.' They are all snobs who look down on and patronize the 'simple' Italians. The exceptions are the Emersons and Lucy, the former because they are still open to learning and do not feel superior to the Italians, and the latter because something in her youthful innocence responds to the beauty and passions of Italy.

In Part Two we see the suffocating effect of rural and London middle class society. Everyone behaves properly, and no one ever has any fun. Lucy almost gets herself talked into marrying a man whom she actually despises. The final chapter finds Lucy and George Emerson back in Italy; they have escaped those things which threatened to kill their Hearts and each has found the answer to their questions about life through love of the other. (Ah! The young E. M. Forster was a hopeless romantic!)

Narrative Point of View:
The story is told from the point of view of a third person narrator who is pretty much, but not entirely, omniscient (i.e. all-knowing). The narrator clearly knows what is going on in the Heads and Hearts of *all* of his characters, though he tends to restrict his psychological explanations to Lucy (technically called third person limited perspective). However, he also makes it clear that he does not have control over the feelings and actions of his characters, again particularly Lucy. This introduces an element of comedy when the impotent narrator becomes frustrated by something that Lucy does, or says, or fails to understand. At one point, he actually appeals to the reader to explain to the silly girl the error she is making because he has no power to do so.

Genre:
The novel is a romance. It is often described as Forster's most optimistic book because it has an unambiguously happy ending. (Published in 1908, Forster could not have known that World War I would probably shatter the happiness of Lucy

and George.) Critics often talk of Forster 'tea-tabling' his action. What they mean is that he manages to deal with really important issues in the context of apparently trivial actions and situations. In this, he was a follower of Jane Austen of whom he was a great fan.

Beneath this veneer of lightness, the novel is a sustained and bitter attack on the society of his day. In its way, it is as revolutionary as the shocking sexual theories of Sigmund Freud with which it has much in common

Tone:

The novel is a comedy of manners. It is full of comic situations because the characters do the most absurd things, and full of good jokes because the author is aware of this absurdity whilst his characters are not. The fact that the characters take themselves so seriously adds immensely to the comedy. Of course, the humor is very subtle and, being over a hundred years old, it might not be as clear to the modern reader as it once was, but if you will allow yourself to get into his style, parts of it are hilarious.

Commentary and Guiding Questions

Learning aims:
Through studying this novel, you will:

1. Gain an understanding of the 'classic' English novel;
2. Understand the ways in which the writer manipulates **authorial perspective**;
3. Experience the writer's use of **verbal irony**;
4. See how the writer uses **symbolism** to add meaning to the narrative.

How to Use this Study Guide:

The questions are not designed to test you but to help you to locate and to understand information in the text. They do not normally have simple answers, nor is there always one answer. Consider a range of possibly interpretations - preferably by discussing the questions with others. Disagreement is encouraged!

Notes:
1. Literary terms are printed in bold and underlined. There is a glossary at the back of this guide.
2. I have not given page references because the novel exists in so many different editions.

PART ONE

Chapter One: The Bertolini

Italy has the ability to disturb the narrow-minded British traveler, widening horizons and transforming her. Whilst most of the British effectively cut themselves off from meaningful contact with Italy, Lucy Honeychurch both unconsciously longs for and consciously fears this kind of experience. She is deeply disappointed by the Pension Bertolini, the inside of which is decorated like a room in London, where British social conventions are observed and the guests are protected from the foreign country that is all around them.

Lucy feels all this in a confused sort of way, for she is very young and naïve and not brave enough to trust her natural impulses. She is a typical girl of the English upper-middle class, often caught between the 'delicacy' she had been taught to value and an inner sense of what is 'beautiful'. Part of her wants to go out into Italy and feel it as richly as she can, away from the safety of British décor and sensibilities. Her longing for a room with a view is a **metaphor** for her desire to connect with Italy and with the new experiences which the country offers. The window opening out into the city of Florence **symbolizes** Lucy's

A Room with a View by E. M. Forster

desire to see a world whose values conflict radically with those of the England in which she has been raised; Italy is a world at once enticing and terrifying.

In *A Room with a View*, Forster generally adopts the perspective of **omniscient** (all-knowing) **narrator**. [But see question 24 later for an interesting limitation which Forster deliberately imposed upon himself.] Forster provides the reader with constant insight into Lucy's feelings, revealing the conflict between the conventionality of her ideas and the subconscious impulses towards a more life-affirming philosophy. The reader is never in any doubt about the direction Forster wishes Lucy to take, nor is there any real doubt that Lucy will eventually make the right decision.

1. The English abroad are absurdly *comic*. How does Forster convey this absurdity? Examine:

    * the description of the Pension Bertolini;

    * the conventions which govern their behavior to each other;

    * their attitude to Italy.

2. In what ways are the Emersons different from the other tourists at the pension?

3. What evidence does Forster provide that Lucy Honeychurch is, on the one hand, very much influenced in her opinions by her respectable elders (particularly Miss Bartlett) and, on the other hand, has the potential to be very rebellious against the respectable conventions of her elders?

4. What is meant by the terms "beauty" and "delicacy" as they are used by the characters in this chapter? What different views are expressed about the relationship of the two?

5. "Miss Bartlett, the poor relation who thinks she is acting from duty, is really acting from a kind of malice - ... trying to recruit the unawakened heroine into 'the armies of the benighted, who follow neither the heart nor the brain'" (Lionel Trilling). What do we learn of the character of Miss Bartlett to support this view?

6. The **narrative** is sprinkled with rather good jokes that exploit a **paradoxical irony** in which Jane Austen would have delighted. Here are two examples:

    "'It is so difficult - at least I find it difficult - to understand people who speak the truth' [Mr. Beebe said]."

    "'He seems to see good in everyone. No one would take him for a clergyman' [Lucy said]."

    Explain the **ironic humor** of these comments and find at least one other example.

A Study Guide

Chapter Two: In Santa Croce With No Baedeker

Have you ever used a guidebook when visiting a place with which you were not familiar? They are very useful - particularly if you have to do a lot in a very short time. However, they are also dangerous because they judge for you what it worth seeing and what is not worth seeing; they also dictate how you should react to what you see. If you are not careful, you end up judging everything through the eyes of the guidebook and not through your own eyes.

7. The chapter opens with a description of Lucy looking out of her window to Italy that concludes with the **authorial comment**: "Over such trivialities as these many a valuable hour may slip away, and the traveler who has gone to Italy to study the tactile values of Giotto, or the corruption of the Papacy, may return remembering nothing but the blue sky and the man and women who live under it." How is it made clear that the reader that this comment is intended to be understood as **ironic**?

8. What was (and still is) a Baedeker? Why do the English tourists rely so much on their Baedeker? How does Forster show the absurdity of this reliance?

9. Miss Lavish (note in passing the comic significance of the name!) is variously described as "clever," "'a real Radical'" and someone who can show Lucy "'the True Italy.'" In fact, Forster uses this character as an example of false rebelliousness. She is ultimately as snobby and 'precious' as everyone else, and her fake radicalism tends to reinforce stuffy conventions rather than challenge them. How does Forster make this clear?

10. Throughout the chapter, Lucy has several moments of spontaneous joy and beauty. Identify these. How are they different from her viewing of the artistic masterpieces approved by Baedeker?

11. Lucy determines that she will be "beautiful rather than delicate" towards the Emersons. What is the difference between being "beautiful" and being "delicate"? How well does she succeed in her determination?

12. Why is Mr. Eager (the name is again of comic significance!) so offended by the comments of Mr. Emerson? Comment on the **irony** of the scraps of Mr. Eager's lecture which come "floating round the partition wall."

13. What have we learnt in the first two chapters of the reasons for George's unhappiness?

14. What does Mr. Emerson mean when he tells Lucy, "'You are inclined to get muddled'"?

A Room with a View by E. M. Forster

Chapter Three: Music, Violets, and the Letter S

Have you ever said or done the *wrong* thing? Remember how everyone looked at you disapprovingly?

Sometimes we do the wrong thing out of the very best motives, which is what happens in this chapter. People are then confused because they do not know whether to disapprove of the action or to approve of it because the intention was good.

15. In what sense is the world of music, which Lucy enters when she plays the piano, "a more solid world" than the world of "everyday life"?

16. Explain Mr. Beebe's attitude to Lucy's playing. What is the "illogical element in Miss Honeychurch" which he has discovered?

17. "Miss Bartlett might reveal unknown depths of strangeness, though not, perhaps, of meaning." For what action of Charlotte's very near the end of the novel does Mr. Beebe's insight prepare us? (Of course, this question only makes sense if you are reading the book for the second time. If you are reading it for the first time, just be aware that the statement **foreshadows** a very surprising idea that George has about Miss Bartlett right at the end of the novel.)

18. Mr. Beebe says of the Italians: "... they know what we want before we know it ourselves... They read our thoughts, they foretell our desires." How does this help us to understand the meeting of Lucy with George amongst the violets which forms the climax of the first part of the novel? (Another piece of **foreshadowing**. Don't forget it!)

19. Forster comments that Miss Alan's account of Miss Lavish has "unexpected beauty." What is it about Miss Alan's attitude to Miss Lavish that produces beauty?

20. What social blunders of Mr. Emerson's does Miss Alan recount to Lucy? How does Forster make these revelations *comic*?

21. Examine Mr. Beebe's reaction to both the failure of his "gentle effort to introduce the Emersons into Bertolini society" and to Lucy's decision to go out.

Chapter Four: Fourth Chapter

The following quotation may help to clarify the significance of the incident that forms the center of this chapter:

'Death,' wrote E. M. Forster in *Howards End*, 'destroys a man, but the idea of   death saves him.' The imaginative realization of death, that is, can clarify one's view of life. It can make the parts fall into a meaningful pattern; it can save one, sometimes, from the kind of blindness born of concentrated egoism that theologians have called the worst of the sins, pride. (Hyatt Howe Waggoner)

22. Why do you think that Forster gives this chapter its rather obvious title?

23. With what aspects of her conventional life is Lucy impatient at the start of this chapter? How does she express her rebellion? What are the self-imposed limits of this rebellion?

24. Forster writes this novel in **third person, limited perspective**. The only two characters whose deepest thoughts he does not communicate are George and Mr. Emerson, both of whom the reader must judge only from Forster's descriptions of what they do and say. From what you have read of the novel so far, why do you think that the author makes this choice? How does his choice affect this chapter?

25. As he is dying of a stab wound, Forster says of the Italian, "he bent towards Lucy with a look of interest, as if he had an important message for her." In reality, the Italian has no message for Lucy (How could he have – he doesn't know her and he doesn't speak English!). However, **symbolically**, the Italian does have a very important message for Lucy. What is it?

26. George says that he must face what has happened "'without getting muddled.'" Does he succeed? Explain how the experience which he has shared with Lucy leads him to the tentative conclusion, "'I shall probably want to live … I shall want to live, I say.'"

27. Does Lucy succeed in facing what has happened without getting muddled?

Chapter Five: Possibilities of a Pleasant Outing

Lucy is now in a fix: she has been frightened by the emotions stirred by the experience she has shared with George, but she is equally frightened, in a different way, by the reactions of her polite and proper acquaintances. She decides that the only thing to do is to run away from a situation in which she feels thoroughly uncomfortable.

28. Why does Lucy decline Mr. Beebe's invitation to join his walk up to the Torre del Gallo?

29. What is **ironic** about Lucy's verdict that, "Yesterday had been a muddle"?

30. We learn of Lucy that, "At present her great aim was not to get put into it [Miss Lavish's novel]." Why, in the light of what happens later in the novel, is this very **ironic**? (More **foreshadowing**. Don't forget it!)

A Room with a View by E. M. Forster

31. Explain why Lucy's reaction to Mr. Eager's invitation to a "drive in the hills" is different from the way she would have reacted a "few days ago."

32. Forster comments of Lucy: "She had been a little frightened, both by Miss Lavish and by Mr. Eager, she knew not why ... They were tried by some new test, and they were found wanting." The reader, however, is left in no doubt about why Lucy finds the two so scary or about the nature of the new test. Explain Lucy's reaction to their behavior.

33. What does Mr. Eager's accusation against Mr. Emerson, "'That man murdered his wife!'" tell us of Mr. Eager's character and what do we learn of Lucy from her reactions to the accusation?

34. As she walks home through the Piazza, Lucy passes by a series of statues, which suggest "not the innocence of childhood, nor the glorious bewilderment of youth, but the conscious achievements of maturity. Perseus and Judith, Hercules and Thusnelda, they have done or suffered something, and though they are immortal, immortality has come to them after experience, not before." What do these classical statues **symbolize** in relation to Lucy's emotional growth?

35. Explain Lucy's desire to leave Florence for Rome immediately.

Chapter Six: [They] Drive out in Carriages to See a View ...

The allusions to Phaethon and Persephone help to establish Italy as a world where the gods of the Ancient World still live. Neither Christianity nor Science and Discovery have eliminated Phaethon. The carriage driver is a **metaphor** for the soul of Italy where the sensuality of the Greek myths lives on. He is presented as the brave but reckless driver of the Sun's powerful golden horses, while his girlfriend, Persephone, represents the coming of springtime.

A central **theme** of the novel is the clash between the impulse to passion and the fears and inhibitions that the British have about emotion, sex and the human body. In this chapter, Lucy is forced to experience this clash within herself.

36. "The real event - whatever it was - had taken place, not on the Loggia, but by the river." Explain what "the real event" was and why Lucy finds it so disturbing.

37. In what ways does the narrative make Mr. Eager appear to be an unsympathetic character? What point is Forster making through the disagreement between Mr. Eager and Mr. Emerson over the proper translation of "Non fate guerra al Maggio"? [Consider particularly Mr. Emerson's question, "'Do you suppose there's any difference between Spring in nature and Spring in man? But there we go, praising one and

condemning the other as improper, ashamed that the same laws work eternally through us both.'"]

38. When Mr. Eager separates the driver and his girlfriend, each appeals to Lucy. The narrative asks: "Why should [they] appeal to Lucy?" This is an example of **dramatic irony** because the answer is as obvious to the reader (and to the author, who only pretends not to know) as it is to the driver and his girlfriend. What is it and how has Forster made it obvious?

39. There have been at least two earlier references to violets before Lucy tumbles into the violets at the end of this chapter (one is in Chapter Three and one in this chapter). What are they and why are they important?

40. How does it happen that, when looking for the two clergymen, Lucy is directed by the driver to George? What is remarkable about the driver's final words to Lucy before she meets George?

41. Examine the water **symbolism** in the description of Lucy's encounter with George.

42. Comment on the **symbolism** of the final sentence: "The silence of life had been broken by Miss Bartlett, who stood brown against the view."

Chapter Seven: They Return

The storm through which Lucy drives is a symbol of the storm of emotions within her. Everything would be fine if George could only speak to Lucy, but Charlotte makes sure that that does not happen.

43. What is the nature of the "COMPLICATED GAME" which the English play that afternoon with "scraps of their intelligence"? What does Forster mean by his **authorial comment** that only the driver had played "skillfully" that afternoon, using "the whole of his instinct"? What message had Lucy "received five days before from the lips of a dying man" and how has the driver been able to interpret that message?

44. As so often in this novel, weather is used to **symbolize the state of the action**. Explain the significance of the fact that it is raining so violently.

45. Compare and contrast Mr. Eager's advice to Lucy, "'courage and faith'" with that of the driver, "'courage and love.'"

46. What are the reasons that lead Charlotte to assume that George will disgrace Lucy by speaking about their encounter?

47. What does Forster mean by the **authorial comment**, "Lucy was suffering from the most grievous wrong which this world has yet discovered: diplomatic advantage had been taken of her sincerity, of her craving for sympathy and love"? To ask much the same question more simply: In what

ways does Charlotte succeed in muddling Lucy about her feelings towards George?

PART TWO

Chapter Eight: Medieval

Forster associates Cecil with the medieval that he uses as a **symbol** of the sexless, the repressed, and the humorless. The medieval is the unenlightened Dark Age period that separates the end of the classical world from the rebirth of classical learning in the Renaissance. Italy is, of course, the land of both Roman and the Renaissance.

Forster structures the novel to reflect these three periods of history. Part 1 is in Italy, where Lucy feels the liberating power of a more spontaneous way of life, and meets George. Part 2 deals with Lucy's relationship in England with Cecil whom Forster compares to a Gothic statue. All her life, Lucy has had her decisions made for her. In Italy, she allowed Charlotte to make critical choices for her, and now she seems determined to marry a man who will completely control her. Fittingly, given the choice that Lucy eventually makes, the final chapter of the novel returns to Italy.

48. Comment on the **symbolic *significance*** of the description in the first paragraph. (Remembering the title of the novel might help!)

49. Explain Forster's **extended simile**, "Cecil … [was like] a Gothic statue."

50. How does Mrs. Honeychurch's reaction to the prospect of Cecil marrying Lucy show that she values prevailing social definitions of respectability?

51. What is it about Lucy that attracts Cecil when they meet in Italy? Consider the **dramatic irony** of Cecil's verdict that, "Italy worked some marvel in her." (Remember that Lucy had just run away from George feeling that she had allowed herself to do something terrible.)

52. What exactly is wrong with Cecil and how is this shown in the narrative?

53. What does Forster mean by his concluding **authorial comment**, "If they were hypocrites they did not know it, and their hypocrisy had every chance of setting and becoming true."

Chapter Nine: Lucy as a Work of Art

Cecil's dissatisfaction with the people around whom Lucy has grown up is a rejection of an important part of her. He wants to remake her into something as urban and critical as himself; he seeks to shape her as he would shape a painting or a sculpture. He does not want her to develop her own opinions but to take on his. This is particularly unfortunate since Italy has awoken in Lucy greater tolerance of those who might be socially and culturally inferior to her.

54. What does Cecil's reaction to the garden-party and to Sir Harry add to our understanding of his character?

55. Cecil and Mr. Beebe tend to view Lucy as a project in progress. How does each see her future development?

56. Account for Lucy's "incongruous … moral outburst over Mr. Eager." What is significant about Cecil's reaction to it?

57. Examine the conversation between Lucy and Cecil which centers around Cecil's statement:

> "'I have got an idea - I dare say wrongly - that you feel more at home with me in a room.'"

How does this exchange relate to the central **themes and symbols** of the novel?

58. What does Cecil's request for a kiss and his reflection on his part in the experience add to our understanding of his character?

59. What do we learn from the chapter about the importance of social class in the world of Summer Street and Windy Corner?

60. Account for the title of the chapter.

Chapter Ten: Cecil as a Humorist

Cecil despises people whom he judges to be uneducated, unrefined, and uncultured. He has taken a particular dislike to the pretentious Sir Harry and has no hesitation in playing a practical joke on him, even though in the process he hurts Lucy and uses the Emersons.

61. Mrs. Honeychurch is a social snob. What evidence do we have of this and how does Forster make it clear that **ironically** she, of all people, should feel no snobbery?

62. Italy brought Cecil and Lucy together, but **ironically** in its different effect upon each of them also made it inevitable that they could never remain together. How is this explained in the first few paragraphs of the chapter?

63. "Hitherto truth had come to her [Lucy] naturally." Why has Lucy's natural tendency to tell the truth abandoned her, and in what ways is she made to suffer for it in this chapter?

64. Explain Cecil's reason for getting the Emersons to move into the district. Why is Lucy so annoyed with him for doing it? How is his action an example of **dramatic irony**?

Chapter Eleven: In Mrs. Vyse's Well-appointed Flat

Lucy thinks that she should try to be more like the Vyses (note again the significance of the name) who are cultured and intellectual people and part of London society. She sees this kind of self-transformation as improving her character. However, the environment of fashionable London stifles her passion. The Vyses are planning to transform her into a woman acceptable to their sterile world.

The dream (nightmare) which Lucy suffers at the end of the chapter is very Freudian: her subconscious is trying to tell her something.

65. How, at the start of this chapter, does Lucy use logic to persuade herself that her feelings are not important?

66. Comment on the way Forster uses **comedy** as a means of showing the reader how unsatisfactory the Vyses and their friends are.

67. Examine the **symbolic** *significances* of:

- Lucy's decision to play Schumann;
- Lucy's nightmare;
- the final sentence of the chapter.

Chapter Twelve: Twelfth Chapter

It is Forster's little joke to give the most important chapter in each Part the blandest title. What happens at the lake is literally magical. It is as though we are momentarily transported back to the Celtic Britain of enchanted woods and fairies. (Realists beware!)

68. Mr. Emerson has hand-painted the inscription, "Mistrust all enterprises that require new clothes" on his wardrobe. (This is a paraphrase of the famous quote from Henry David Thoreau, "Beware all enterprises which require new clothes" [Walden, Economy, 1854]. Mr. Emerson is named for the American philosopher Ralph Waldo Emerson.) What do clothes **symbolize** for Mr. Emerson, and how does this quotation add to your understanding of his philosophy of life?

69. Compare George's reaction to Freddy's impulsive invitation to "'Come and have a bathe'" with Cecil's attitude to tennis throughout the novel. Freddy

keeps asking George if he really means to go swimming. How does this show an important difference between the two young men?

70. How is each of the men affected by bathing naked in the pool and by being discovered doing so?

71. How is this swimming incident related to:

- Lucy's meeting with George in the "pools" of violets;

- Mr. Emerson's views expressed earlier in this chapter on The Garden of Eden?

72. Comment on Cecil's behavior at the pool.

73. What do you notice about the way in which Forster presents Lucy's reaction to the incident? How is his use of **third person, limited perspective** here different from the way Forster uses it in the rest of the novel? Why do you think that Forster made this change?

74. What **symbolic** *significance* does the final paragraph of the chapter give to the experience of swimming in the pool?

Chapter Thirteen: How Miss Bartlett's Boiler was so Tiresome

Lucy's world is revealed to be absolutely tiresome, but she seemed to be trapped in it. Given a few years, she will *become* Charlotte Bartlett.

75. How do the first two paragraphs show us Lucy's failure to control her heart?

76. When Lucy tells Freddy not to invite the Emersons to Windy Corner "'with all this muddle'" to what is she referring? Lucy uses the word "muddle." To what is Forster referring?

77. What is it about Cecil's behavior that Mrs. Honeychurch finds objectionable? (Comment on the significance of Freddy's comment on Charlotte, "'I only meant how jolly kind she seemed.'")

Chapter Fourteen: How Lucy Faced the External Situation Bravely

It is time for Lucy to face an internal situation bravely! She loves George - will someone please tell her?

78. What is implied by the title of this chapter? How does Forster make in clear in the opening paragraphs that Lucy is in a "muddle" over her feelings for Cecil and for George? (Comment in particular about the **authorial perspective** implicit in the following, "[Lucy] loved Cecil; George made her nervous; will the reader explain to her that the phrases should have been reversed?")

79. Why is Charlotte so nervous about Cecil learning about the incident among the violets from "'some other source'"?

80. What exactly is the "unfortunate slip" that Lucy makes in her "rather ... good speech"? Comment on Forster's **tone** in this comment.

Chapter Fifteen: The Disaster Within

Lucy is literally withering away in front of our eyes! Even worse, from her point of view, the lies she has told to cover her feelings are unraveling.

81. Forster continues his ***figurative use*** of classical mythology in the description, "The sun rose higher on its journey, guided, not by Phaethon, but by Apollo, competent, unswerving, divine." Remembering that the Italian driver who guided Lucy and George to their first kiss was figuratively referred to as Phaethon (who drove his father's horses and the chariot carrying the sun to disaster), comment on the author's use of **symbolism** here.

82. When Lucy appears, Forster comments, "Her new cerise dress has been a failure, and makes her look tawdry and wan." In the context of the **symbolism** of clothes in the novel so far, what is Forster saying about Lucy in this description? (Comment particularly on the **simile** that compares Lucy to "a brave child when he is trying not to cry."]

83. In this, and the previous chapter, how does Forster **foreshadow** the climax of the reading by Cecil of Miss Lavish's account of the incident in the violets?

84. Comment on the **dramatic irony** of Lucy's thought, "Only three English people knew of it…"

85. Forster's **authorial comment**, "Thus she interpreted her joy" suggests that Lucy is misinterpreting her joy. Explain the "muddle" into which she has fallen.

86. Trace Lucy's growing discontent with Cecil and her growing (but suppressed) attraction to George. Lucy makes another "unfortunate slip" when George describes meeting Miss Lavish. What is it?

87. Contrast the attitudes to tennis of George and Cecil.

Chapter Sixteen: Lying to George

George does something beautiful but indelicate - he kisses the girl he loves. All very improper given the morals of the day. To defend George from the accusation that he is forcing himself upon Lucy, Forster has made it abundantly clear that Lucy also loves George and that she wants to be kissed. George knows this. The author and the reader know this. In fact, the only person involved who pretends not to know it is Lucy.

88. Comment on the **verbal irony** of the opening sentence of the chapter.

89. What reasons can you suggest for Charlotte's refusal to talk to George for Lucy?

90. What are George's objections to Cecil as a potential husband for Lucy? What is George's conception of the relationship that he wants with Lucy? (Comment in particular on George's admission, "'I'm the same kind of brute at bottom. This desire to govern a woman - it lies very deep, and men and women must fight it together before they shall enter the garden.'")

91. Examine the **symbolic** *significance* of the description of nature on Lucy's return to "the open air."

92. What particular incident prompts Lucy to break off her engagement with Cecil?

Chapter Seventeen: Lying to Cecil

Actually, a lot of what Lucy says to Cecil is absolutely true. There is really only one lie, but it is a whopper!

93. Comment on Lucy's remark: "'I am forgetting all that I learnt there [i.e., in Italy].'" What does Lucy intend Cecil to understand by the remark? What does Forster intend the reader to understand?

94. At various points of their interview, Forster indicates that Lucy gets very angry ("more angry ... kindling once more ... indignantly ... irritation increased ... crossly"). Explain this anger in Lucy?

95. Summarize Lucy's views on the inadequacies in Cecil's character. Account for the similarity between what she says and what George said in the previous chapter. Why do you think that Forster makes Cecil act so apparently out of character in his reaction?

96. What exactly are the lies that Lucy tells in this chapter? Explain Forster's **metaphor** of "the vast armies of the benighted." Explain the significance of the final sentence.

Chapter Eighteen: Lying to Mr. Beebe, Mrs. Honeychurch, Freddy ...

Just as Lucy tried to run away from her problems in Florence by asking Charlotte if they could go immediately to Rome, so she now discovers that she has always longed to go to Constantinople, or Athens, or wherever it is that the Miss Allens are going.

97. What evidence do we have that Cecil has gained some self-knowledge from his interview with Lucy and has (at least temporarily) changed for the better?

98. What is the **symbolic** *significance* of Forster's description of the disorder caused by the storm in the garden at Windy Corner and Mrs. Honeychurch's attempts to restore order to the chaos?

99. In what ways do Lucy's actions in this chapter prove that she is indeed "marching in the armies of darkness"? What lies does she tell?

100. Why is Charlotte so anxious that Lucy should get away from Windy Corner?

101. The character of Mr. Beebe develops in unexpected ways in this chapter. Initially, he instinctively knows that Lucy's plan to escape to Greece is a mistake: "'It's all - I can't explain – it's wrong.'" [Which, of course, it is!] Why, then, does he end up supporting the scheme? [Mr. Beebe is such an attractive character in the early chapters of the book that it is easy to overlook the fact that, even there, he is yet another male character with plans for Lucy. His admiration for her passionate playing of the piano does not, in fact, extend to a desire that she should live her life passionately. He is far wiser and kinder than is Cecil, but he feels that Lucy would be happiest choosing to live in celibacy as he has done. Comment particularly on the **ironic simile** that Forster uses to account for the rector's change of mind, "His belief in celibacy, so reticent, so carefully concealed beneath his tolerance and culture, now came to the surface and expanded like some delicate flower."]

102. Throughout the novel, the music that Lucy plays is **symbolically** *significant*. What is the significant about her playing in this chapter? Examine closely the words of the song that Forster has her singing at the end of the chapter? Comment on the **unconscious irony** of Mr. Beebe's judgment that it is "'a beautiful song and a wise one.'"

103. The **symbolism** of darkness is significant in the chapter. Comment on each of the following:

    - "'... we shall have darkness... The darkness last night was appalling'";
    - "The darkness was coming on";
    - "They [Charlotte and Beebe] hurried home through a world of black and grey";
    - "Windy Corner lay poised below him [Beebe] - now as a beacon in the roaring tides of darkness."

A Study Guide

Chapter Nineteen: Lying to Mr. Emerson

This is a beautiful chapter. Forster uses Mr. Emerson as a mouthpiece for what it is that he wants to say (this *is* a novel of ideas), and the result is over-long - even Mr. Emerson admits that. But what he says is wonderful and true.

Here is my favorite sentence in all literature, "'Marry him [George]; it's one of the moments for which the world was made.'" Perfect!

104. What indications do we get in Forster's account of Lucy's trip to London to meet the Miss Alans that Lucy is "one who had deliberately warped the brain"?

105. What point is Forster's making by having Mrs. Honeychurch draw attention to the growing similarity between Lucy and Charlotte?

106. What can we deduce about Charlotte's request to go to church?

107. Early in their conversation, Lucy says of George that in kissing her he "'behaved *abominably.*'" What is the significance of the fact that Forster has Lucy repeat a word that she first used on page 18? (What is the significance of the fact that the author expects the reader to remember?)

108. Contrast Mr. Emerson's view of love and marriage with that of Mr. Beebe.

109. At the point where he hears Mr. Emerson say that Lucy has loved George all along, what do you notice about the way Forster describes Mr. Beebe and makes him act? (Comment particularly on the **metaphor** "A long black column.")

110. What exactly does Lucy learn from Mr. Emerson?

Chapter Twenty: The End of the Middle Ages

Lucy and George have to escape England (at least temporarily) in order to be themselves. Lucy can now live her life the way she plays Beethoven - on the side of Victory. George no longer needs the universe to make sense - his love for Lucy and her love for him makes his life meaningful.

111. Explain the **symbolic** *significance* of the title of this chapter.

112. Lucy and George have been rejected by all of Lucy's friends and family. Why?

113. In Chapter 19, Mrs. Honeychurch accuses Lucy of having grown tired of Windy Corner "and our dear view." What details in this chapter confirm that she was actually right?

A Room with a View by E. M. Forster

114. Which details of Forster's description prove that Mr. Emerson "had robbed the body of its taint ... shown her the holiness of direct desire"?

115. What startling possibility about Charlotte's motives emerges?

A Study Guide

A Room with a View Reading Quiz for Part 1 Chapters 1 & 2

1. Lucy Honeychurch lives in the village of: Summer _____
   a) Meadow   b) Glade   c) Street   d) Way

2. Lucy decides that Mr. Emerson is:
   a) Rude   b) Nice   c) Good   d) Polite

3. The first thing that Charlotte does when she enters her room to go to bed is:
   a) Take down the question mark b) Unpack her cases
   c) Write a note to Lucy's mother d) Fasten the window-shutters

4. When she is looking out of her window the next morning, Lucy sees all of the following except:
   a) A tramcar   b) Some white bullocks
   c) A group of soldiers   d) A man herding sheep

5. Lucy sets out to explore Florence with:
   a) Charlotte   b) Mr. Beebe
   c) Miss Lavish   d) Miss Allen

6. Because they are beginning to feel hungry, Lucy and her companion purchase some:
   a) Hot chestnut paste   b) Italian sausage
   c) Pizza   d) Olives

7. Having been abandoned by her companion, Lucy enters the church of:
   a) Santa Croce   b) Santa Gordia
   c) Santa Marie   d) Santa Paula

8. In the church, Lucy sees all of the following except:
   a) Mr. Beebe   b) Mr. Emerson
   c) Rev. Eager   d) Miss Bartlett

9. In the church, Lucy particularly want to see the wall paintings by:
   a) Leonardo   b) Raphael
   c) Giotto   d) Archimboldo

10. When he is talking to Lucy, Mr. Emerson warns her against
    a) Getting confused   b) Getting mixed up
    c) Getting muddled   d) Getting embarrassed

11. Mr. Emerson asks Lucy to:
    a) Fall in love with George   b) Try and understand George
    c) Be nice to George   d) Avoid talking to George

12. At the <u>end</u> of Chapter two, Mr. Emerson calls Lucy:
    a) A spoilt, rich girl   b) A silly girl
    c) A poor girl   d) A sensible girl

A Room with a View by E. M. Forster

A Room with a View Reading Quiz Part 1 Ch. 7 & Part 2 Ch. 8

1. Which character urges Lucy to have "courage and faith"?
   a) Mr. Beebe
   b) Mr. Emerson
   c) Mr. Eager
   d) The Italian driver

2. In order to secure the silence of the driver over the kiss, Lucy "said, 'Silenzio!' and offered him a franc."
   a) True
   b) False

3. The morning after the incident of the picnic, Charlotte and Lucy leave for:
   a) Venice
   b) Milan
   c) Rome
   d) Naples

4. Which character said, "Mr. Vyse is an ideal bachelor"?
   a) Mr. Emerson
   b) Mr. Beebe
   c) Freddie
   d) Mr. Eager

5. Windy Corner is built on the range that overlooks:
   a) The Sussex Weald
   b) The Surrey Hills

6. Forster compares Cecil to:
   a) A Gothic statue
   b) A Greek statue

7. The "semi-detached villas that have been run up opposite the church" are called:
   a) Cissie and Alfred
   b) Cissie and Albert

8. In his diary, Mr. Beebe has a sketch of Lucy as a:
   a) dog on a leash
   b) kite on a string

9. Freddy seems to be studying:
   a) Physics
   b) Chemistry
   c) Biology
   d) Botany

A Room with a View Reading Quiz for Part 2 Chapters 10-12

1. Bumble-puppy, a game that Lucy plays with Minnie Beebe, is a form of:
   a) Tennis   b) Badminton   c) Soccer   d) Golf

2. Freddie takes to calling Cecil:
   a) Fiancé   b) Fiasco

   3. Sir Harry Otway decides to let one of the villas to the Emersons on the recommendation of:
   a) Freddy   b) Mr. Beebe   c) Lucy d) Cecil

4. Lucy hears the name of the people to whom Sir Harry has let the villas from:
   a) Mrs. Honeychurch b) Charlotte
   c) Mr. Beebe   d) Freddie

5. Cecil tells Lucy that he met the Emersons:
   a) At a lecture   b) In a museum
   c) In an art gallery   d) At a music concert

6. One of the following met George Emerson in Summer Street and passed the information to Lucy:
   a) Miss Alan   b) Miss Lavish
   c) Miss Bartlett   d) Mr. Beebe

7. The first night of Lucy's visit to Mrs. Vyse's flat in London is ruined by:
   a) A disagreement with Cecil b) A nightmare

8. When Freddie first asked George to "Come and have a bathe," George replies:
   a) "Oh, I don't think so"   b) "Oh, not today"
   c) "Oh, certainly"   d) "Oh, all right"

9. Of the three gentlemen, one is the last to enter the pool:
   a) Mr. Beebe   b) George   c) Freddie

10. Just after he more or less falls into the pool, George says:
    a) "Water's wonderful"   b) "Water's not so bad"

11. Face to face with a partly naked George, Mrs. Honeychurch suggests to Lucy that they:
    a) Pretend he is not there at allb) Bow to him
    c) Blame Freddie   d) Walk away as quickly as possible

A Room with a View by E. M. Forster

A Room with a View **Reading Quiz for Part 2 Chapters 17-20**

1. The thing that Lucy says finally leads her to break her engagement with Cecil is:

   a) His reading Miss Lavish's book   b) George kissing Lucy
   c) His refusal to play tennis   d) What George says about Cecil

2. After Lucy has broken off her engagement with Cecil, he asks her:

   a) To kiss him one final time   b) To play Beethoven
   c) To shake hands   d) Not to tell anyone until he leaves

3. Lucy tries to persuade her mother to let her go away from Windy Corner with the Miss Alans by saying that she:

   a) must get away from George   b) must avoid gossip
   c) has always longed to visit Greece d) longs to see the Miss Alans again

4. On her trip to London with her mother to meet the Miss Alans, Lucy purchases:

   a) Some digestive bread   b) A mackintosh square
   c) A Baedeker   d) A book on Greek sculpture

5. On the way home from London, Mrs. Honeychurch tells Lucy that Lucy increasingly reminds her of:

   a) Cecil   b) Her father   c) Freddie   d) Charlotte

6. Lucy meets Mr. Emerson in Mr. Beebe's house because of:

   a) Mr. Beebe b) Charlotte   c) Mrs. Honeychurch   d) Powell

7. When Mr. Emerson tells Mr. Beebe that Lucy loves George, Mr. Beebe says that it is:

   a) "Wonderful, wonderful."   b) "Sad, sad."
   c) "Excellent, excellent."   d) "Lamentable, lamentable."

8. In the final chapter, when Lucy and George have returned to Florence, Lucy is reading a letter from:

   a) Freddie   b) Charlotte c) Her mother   d) Mr. Beebe

9. Whilst they talk, Lucy is:

   a) Mending a sock   b) Mending a shirt

10. Right at the end of the novel, George comes up with the remarkable idea that:

   a) Mrs. Honeychurch wanted them to marry all along
   b) Mr. Beebe wanted them to marry all along
   c) Mr. Emerson wanted them to marry all along
   d) Miss Bartlett wanted them to marry all along

Reading Quiz Answers

For Part 1 Chapters 1 & 2
1. c   2. b   3. d   4. d   5. c   6. a   7. a   8. a   9. c   10. c
11. b   12. c

For Part 1 Ch. 7 & Part 2 Ch. 8
1. c   2. b   3. c   4. b   5. a   6. a   7. b   8. b   9. d

For Part 2 Chapters 10-12
1. a   2. b   3. d   4. d   5. c   6. b   7. b   8. d   9. a   10. b
11. b

For Part 2 Chapters 17-20
1. c   2. c   3. c   4. c   5. d   6. b   7. d   8. a   9. a   10. d

A Room with a View by E. M. Forster

Literary terms activity

As you use each term in the study guide, fill in the definition of the term and include an example from the text to show how it is used. The first definition is supplied. Find an example in the text to complete it.

Term	Definition
	Example
authorial (or narrator's) perspective	*the narrator's view of events (typically first-person)*
foreshadow	
irony, ironic, ironically	
irony, dramatic	
irony, unconscious	
irony, verbal	

A Study Guide

Term	Definition
	Example
metaphor	
narrator	
paradoxical	
simile	
simile, extended	
symbol, symbolic, symbolism, symbolize:	

A Room with a View by E. M. Forster

Term	Definition
	Example
theme:	
third person limited perspective	

A Study Guide

Literary terms definitions

NOTE Not all of these terms may be relevant to this particular study guide

Allegorical: a story in which the characters, their actions and the settings represent abstract ideas (often moral ideas) or historical/ political events.

Ambiguous, ambiguity: when a statement is unclear in meaning- ambiguity may be deliberate or accidental

Analogy: a comparison which treats two things as identical in one or more specified ways

Antagonist: an opposing character or force to the protagonist

Antithesis: the complete opposite of something

Authorial comment: when the writer addresses the reader directly (not to be confused with the narrator doing so.)

Climax: the conflict to which the action has been building since the start of the play or story.

Colloquialism: the casual, informal mainly spoken language of ordinary people - often called" slang".

Comic hyperbole: deliberately inflated, extravagant language used for comic effect

Comic Inversion: reversing the normal order of things for comic effect

Connotation: the ideas, feelings and associations generated by a word or phrase

Couplet: two lines of poetry whether rhymed of unrhymed.

Dark comedy: comedy which has a serious implication

Dialogue: a conversation between two or more people in direct speech

Diction: the writer's choice of words in order to create a particular effect

Dramatic function or purpose: some characters and plot devices in plays are used by the author for specific purposes necessary to the action

Dramatic significance: importance of an act, speech, or character in the context of the play itself

Equivocation: saying something which is capable of two interpretations with the intention of misrepresenting the truth

Euphemism: a polite word for an ugly truth for example, a person is said to be sleeping when they are actually dead

Fallacy: a misconception resulting from incorrect reasoning

First person: first person singular is "I" and plural is "we"

Foreshadow: a statement or action which gives the reader a hint of what is likely to happen later in the narrative

Form of speech: the register in which speech is written - the diction reflects the character

Frame narrative: a story within which the main narrative is placed

A Room with a View by E. M. Forster

Genre: the type of literature into which a particular text falls (e.g. drama, poetry, novel)

Hubris: pride- in Greek tragedy it is the hero's belief that he can challenge the will of the gods.

Hyperbole: exaggeration designed to create a particular effect

Image, imagery: figurative language such as simile, metaphor, personification etc., or a description which conjures u a particularly vivid picture

Imply, implication: when the text suggests to the reader a meaning which it does not actually state

Infer, inference: the reader's act of going beyond what is stated in the text to draw conclusions

Irony, ironic: a form of humor which undercuts the apparent meaning of a statement

> *Conscious irony:* irony used deliberately by a writer or character

> *Unconscious irony:* a statement or action which has significance for the reader of which the character is unaware

> *Dramatic irony*: when an action has an important significance that is obvious to the reader but not to one or more of the characters

> *Tragic irony:* when a character says (or does) something which will have a serious, even fatal, consequence for him/ her. The audience is aware of the error, but the character is not.

> *Verbal irony*: the conscious use of particular words which are appropriate to what is being said

Juxtaposition: literally putting two things side by side for purposes of comparison and/ or contrast

Literal: the surface level of a statement

Machiavellian: a person for whom the end justifies the means - a devious, manipulative, character whose only concern is his/ her own good

Malapropism: the unconscious misuse of language by a character so that key words are replaced by similar sounding words, which make no sense in the context in which they are used, the effect being unintentionally comic

Melodramatic: action and/or dialogue that is inflated or extravagant- frequently used for comic effect

Metaphor, metaphorical: the description of one thing by direct comparison with another (e.g. the coal-black night)

> *Extended metaphor: a comparison which is developed at length*

Microcosm: literally 'the world is little' - a situation which reflects truths about the world in general

Mood: the feelings and emotions contained in and/ or produced by a work of art (text, painting, music, etc.)

Motif: a frequently repeated idea, image or situation

A Study Guide

Motivation: why a character acts as he/ she does- in modern literature motivation is seen as psychological

Narrates, narrator: the voice that the reader hears in the text

> *Frame narrative /story:* a story within which the main story is told (e.g. "heart of darkness" by Conrad begins with five men on a boat in the Thames and then one of them tells the story of his experiences on the river Congo)

Oxymoron: the juxtaposition of two terms normally thought of as opposite (e.g. the silent scream)

Parable: a story with a moral lesson (e.g. the Good Samaritan)

Paradox, paradoxical: a statement or situation which appears self-contradictory and therefore absurd

Pathos: is pity, or rather the ability of a text to make the audience or reader feel pity

Perspective: point of view from which a story, or an incident within a story, is told

Personified, personification: a simile or metaphor in which an inanimate object or abstract idea is described by comparison with a human

Plot: a chain of events linked by cause and effect

Prologue: an introduction which gives a lead-in to the main story

Protagonist: the character who initiates the action and is most likely to have the sympathy of the audience

Pun: a deliberate play on words where a particular word has two or more meanings both appropriate in some way to what is being said

Realism: a text that describes the action in a way that appears to reflect life

Rhetoric: the art of public speaking and more specifically the techniques which make speaking and writing effective

Rhetorical device: any use of language designed to make the expression of ideas more effective (e.g. repetition, imagery, alliteration, etc.)

Rhyming couplets: two consecutive lines of poetry ending in a full rhyme

Rhythm: literally the 'musical beat' of the words. In good writing, the rhythm of the words is clearly appropriate to what the words describe, so the rhythm is a part of the total meaning of the words

Role: means function- characters in plays (particularly minor characters) frequently have specific functions

Sarcasm: stronger than irony - it involves a deliberate attack on a person or idea with the intention of mocking

Satire, Satiric; the use of comedy to criticize attack, belittle, or humiliate- more extreme than irony

Setting: the environment in which the narrative (or part of the narrative) takes place

Simile: a description of one thing by explicit comparison with another (e.g. my love is like a red, red rose)

A Room with a View by E. M. Forster

Extended simile: a comparison which is developed at length

Soliloquy: where a character in a play, normally alone on the stage, directly addresses the audience. By convention, a character is truthful in a soliloquy, though they may, of course be wrong or self-deceiving

Style: the way in which a writer chooses to express him/ herself. Style is a vital aspect of meaning since how something is expressed can crucially affect what is being written or spoken

Suspense: the building of tension in the reader

Symbol, symbolic, symbolism, symbolize: a physical object which comes to represent an abstract idea (e.g. the sun may symbolize life)

Themes: important concepts, beliefs and ideas explored and presented in a text

Third person: third person singular is "he/ she/ it" and plural is "they" - authors often write novels in the third person

Tone: literally the sound of a text - How words sound (either in the mouth of an actor or the head of a reader) can crucially affect meaning

Tragic: King Richard III and Macbeth are both murderous tyrants, yet only Macbeth is a *tragic* figure. Why? Because Macbeth has the potential to be great, recognizes the error he has made and all that he has lost in making it, and dies bravely in a way that seems to accept the justice of the punishment.

A Study Guide

Oral and Written Commentaries: The Close Reading Process

The emphasis of the study of texts is to understand how the words on the page create meaning. Close reading of a text centers on three basic questions:

- *What does the writer say?* (This is a question about meaning and content.)
- *How does the writer say it?* (This is a question about how style contributes to meaning.)
- *How effectively do the words and structures chosen convey the writer's meaning?* (This is an evaluative question.)

There are obvious differences between reading prose, drama and poetry, between reading whole texts and reading short excerpts, between reading expository discourse and imaginative narrative. Therefore, no single approach will suit all texts. Responding to literature cannot be reduced to a formula. However, the following series of questions offer a basic approach to close reading.

What? Why? (subject, situation, purpose)
- What is happening here?
- What is the intention of the writer?
- Is there a story, characters, plot development?
- Is there an argument and, if so, how is it developed?
- What are the main themes of this piece of writing?

Where? When? (setting)
- What is the landscape created by the writing?
- What are you visualizing as you read it?
- Is the time in which the writing is set important?

Who? To Whom? (voice / speaker / persona / point of view, writer's viewpoint, audience)
- Who is speaking the text?
- What is the relationship between the speaker and the writer?
- For what purposes is the writer using the speaker?
- What role does the text impose on the reader?
- What is the reader's relationship to the speaker?

Patterns (structure / form)
- What patterns are clear in the way the text is structured?
- How do these patterns support the meaning of the text?

Techniques (style)
- What stylistic techniques are used in the text?
- How do these techniques support the meaning of the text?

A Room with a View by E. M. Forster

Tension (conflict / contrast / irony)

- What kinds of tensions or contrast can you find in the text (e.g., between the writer's view and that of the speaker, between the speaker's view and the reader's, between different points of view in the text, between different groups or sets of images, etc.)?

So what? (evaluation)

- How effectively do you feel that the writer has communicated his or her theme(s)?
- What is the dominant effect of this piece of writing? Has the text touched you? How? Why?

The Commentary

A commentary is a written or spoken account of the effects that an author has created in an extract from a longer poetry, drama or prose text. When commenting on an extract from a longer text (or, in the case of poetry, from a larger body of work, perhaps by more than one writer), ***the aim is to analyze how meaning is created by the words on the page.*** Knowledge that you have about the writer's life and beliefs, the cultural background of the text, its socio-historical background, and the place of the extract in the full text or body of work is important only in so far as it is relevant to understanding of the meaning of the extract and how the writer creates that meaning. To put this in another way, you need to show an explicit recognition of the art and craft of the passage and work.

The guiding questions provided will identify for you key issues, literary devices, or themes within the extract. Responding to these questions will give your commentary a central thesis. You then have to exemplify or argue your thesis through a detailed analysis of the extract. Avoid a line by line paraphrase or a series of unconnected points.

The features of an effective commentary are:

- secure understanding of the content and themes of the text;
- a clearly stated thesis which defines the approach that you will take;
- the clear organization of points;
- understanding and appropriate use of literary techniques;
- emphasis on how the writer has used techniques of style to affect the reader;
- a willingness to make a personal response firmly based on the texts;

How to structure a commentary:

1. Begin by briefly situating the extract (i.e., placing the extract in context of the whole text, or, in the case of poetry, of the writer's body of work). This may be done by:

- saying what happened immediately before and immediately after the extract, and how the extract fits into the plot structure of the full text;
- explaining the relationship of the extract to the themes of the whole text;
- placing the extract in its genre (satire, ode, fictional journey, sonnet, comic drama, etc.) and showing awareness of the nature and conventions of that genre;
- placing a poem in relation to the writer's other poems in terms of the date it was written and the poet's concerns at that point in his or her writing career.

2. Explain what you take to be the writer's purpose in the extract. To do this:
   - use your knowledge of the whole text to help you to identify the writer's intention in the particular extract – remember that not everything that is in the whole text can be in every extract;
   - explain the ideas and themes of the extract;
   - identify the tone of the extract and how it is produced;
   - speculate on the effect which the writer wants to produce in the reader.

3. Address each guiding question in turn. State the controlling idea (thesis) which will give structure to your response:
   - define the controlling idea of your commentary in abstract terms;
   - explain how you will use it to structure your detailed analysis.

4. Identify the voices that you hear in the text (the speaker /voice, the dialogue of characters) and any role that the reader must take in relation to the speaker:
   - make clear the relationship between the voice in the text and the writer;
   - explain how the writer uses the speaker in the extract to further his artistic purpose.

5. Describe the subject, setting and situation of the extract.
   - explain how these help the writer to achieve his or her purpose;
   - make an evaluative comment on their effectiveness.

6. Analyze the external structures of the extract (i.e., the structuring devises that you can see even before you have read the extract):
   - in poetry consider such structuring devices as verses (stanzas), line length, end-stopped lines, run-on lines (enjambment), etc.;
   - in prose consider sentence length, paragraphing, use of direct speech, variations in print styles, spacing of lines, etc.;
   - in drama consider the use of stage directions, the length of speeches, use of poetry or prose, the distribution of speech amongst the characters, etc.;

- relate the external structures that you identify to the meaning of the extract: how do they help the writer to achieve his or her purpose?
- relate the external structures that you identify to the controlling idea of your commentary.

7. Analyze the significant stylistic features of the extract:
   - select the stylistic features on which you will comment on the basis of your thesis;
   - in your analysis of stylistic features, make clear how they relate to the controlling idea of your commentary;
   - listen for the writer's manipulation of the sound of words (e.g., rhyme, half-rhyme, alliteration, assonance, repetition / parallelism, onomatopoeia, etc.);
   - consider the writers use of imagery (similes, metaphors, personification, symbols, etc.) and any appeal to particular senses;
   - examine the writer's diction (the words which the writer has chosen to use); look for significance in the use of nouns, adjectives, verbs, adverbs, etc.;
   - look for patterns of sound in the writing (rhythm, sentence structures, parallelisms, etc.);
   - comment on any other stylistic devices which contribute to the meaning of the extract.

8. In conclusion (having addressed both guiding questions), restate the dominant effect of the passage on you:
   - say whether or not the extract produced the effect upon you that you feel the writer intended;
   - say why or why not.

Although the method suggested above is a useful starting point, a commentary cannot be reduced to a 'one size fits all' formula. The more confident you get, the more you will feel able to adapt your approach to the demands of a particular extract and (more importantly) what you want to say about it.

A Study Guide

Written or Oral Commentary # 1

1 He returned, and she talked of the murder. Oddly enough, it was an
2 easy topic. She spoke of the Italian character; she became almost
3 garrulous over the incident that had made her faint five minutes
4 before. Being strong physically, she soon overcame the horror of
5 blood. She rose without his assistance, and though wings seemed to
6 flutter inside her, she walked firmly enough towards the Arno.
7 There a cabman signaled to them; they refused him.

8 "And the murderer tried to kiss him, you say -- how very odd
9 Italians are! -- and gave himself up to the police! Mr. Beebe was
10 saying that Italians know everything, but I think they are rather
11 childish. When my cousin and I were at the Pitti yesterday -- What
12 was that?" He had thrown something into the stream.

13 "What did you throw in?"

14 "Things I didn't want," he said crossly.

15 "Mr. Emerson!"

16 "Well?"

17 "Where are the photographs?"

18 He was silent.

19 "I believe it was my photographs that you threw away."

20 "I didn't know what to do with them," he cried, and his voice was
21 that of an anxious boy.

22 Her heart warmed towards him for the first time. "They were
23 covered with blood. There! I'm glad I've told you; and all the time
24 we were making conversation I was wondering what to do with
25 them." He pointed down-stream. "They've gone." The river swirled
26 under the bridge. "I did mind them so, and one is so foolish, it

27 seemed better that they should go out to the sea -- I don't know; I may
28 just mean that they frightened me. "

29 Then the boy verged into a man. "For something tremendous has
30 happened; I must face it without getting muddled. It isn't exactly that a
31 man has died."

32 Something warned Lucy that she must stop him.

33 "It has happened," he repeated, "and I mean to find out what it is."

34 "Mr. Emerson -- "

35 He turned towards her frowning, as if she had disturbed him in some
36 abstract quest.

37 "I want to ask you something before we go in."

38 They were close to their pension. She stopped and leant her elbows
39 against the parapet of the embankment. He did likewise. There is at times
40 a magic in identity of position; it is one of the things that have suggested
41 to us eternal comradeship. She moved her elbows before saying:

42 "I have behaved ridiculously."

43 He was following his own thoughts.

44 "I was never so much ashamed of myself in my life; I cannot think what
45 came over me."

46 "I nearly fainted myself," he said; but she felt that her attitude repelled
47 him.

48 "Well, I owe you a thousand apologies."

49 "Oh, all right."

50 "And -- this is the real point -- you know how silly people are gossiping

51

52   -- ladies especially, I am afraid -- you understand what I mean?"

53   "I'm afraid I don't."

54   "I mean, would you not mention it to any one, my foolish

55   behaviour?"

56   "Your behaviour? Oh, yes, all right -- all right."

57   "Thank you so much. And would you -- "

58   She could not carry her request any further. The river was rushing

59   below them, almost black in the advancing night. He had thrown her

60   photographs into it, and then he had told her the reason. It struck her

61   that it was hopeless to look for chivalry in such a man.

Guiding Questions:

1. How does this passage illustrate Lucy's tendency to get muddled in her thinking?

2. What are the significant differences in the way in which Lucy and George talk to each other in this extract?

A Room with a View by E. M. Forster

Written or Oral Commentary #2:

1   "I want more independence," said Lucy lamely; she knew that she
2   wanted something, and independence is a useful cry; we can always say
3   that we have not got it. She tried to remember her emotions in Florence:
4   those had been sincere and passionate, and had suggested beauty rather
5   than short skirts and latch-keys. But independence was certainly her cue.

6   "Very well. Take your independence and be gone. Rush up and down
7   and round the world, and come back as thin as a lath with the bad food.
8   Despise the house that your father built and the garden that he planted,
9   and our dear view--and then share a flat with another girl."

10   Lucy screwed up her mouth and said: "Perhaps I spoke hastily."

11   "Oh, goodness!" her mother flashed. "How you do remind me of
12   Charlotte Bartlett!"

13   "Charlotte!" flashed Lucy in her turn, pierced at last by a vivid pain.

14   "More every moment."

15   "I don't know what you mean, mother; Charlotte and I are not the very
16   least alike."

17   "Well, I see the likeness. The same eternal worrying, the same taking
18   back of words. You and Charlotte trying to divide two apples among
19   three people last night might be sisters."

20   "What rubbish! And if you dislike Charlotte so, it's rather a pity you
21   asked her to stop. I warned you about her; I begged you, implored you
22   not to, but of course it was not listened to."

23   "There you go."

24   "I beg your pardon?"

25   "Charlotte again, my dear; that's all; her very words."

26   Lucy clenched her teeth. "My point is that you oughtn't to have

27   asked Charlotte to stop. I wish you would keep to the point." And

28   the conversation died off into a wrangle.

29   She and her mother shopped in silence, spoke little in the train, little

30   again in the carriage, which met them at Dorking Station. It had

31   poured all day and as they ascended through the deep Surrey lanes

32   showers of water fell from the over-hanging beech-trees and rattled

33   on the hood. Lucy complained that the hood was stuffy. Leaning

34   forward, she looked out into the steaming dusk, and watched the

35   carriage-lamp pass like search-light over mud and leaves, and reveal

36   nothing beautiful.

37   "The crush when Charlotte gets in will be abominable," she

38   remarked. For they were to pick up Miss Bartlett at Summer Street,

39   where she had been dropped as the carriage went down, to pay a call

40   on Mr. Beebe's old mother. "We shall have to sit three a side,

41   because the trees drop, and yet it isn't raining. Oh, for a little air!"

42   Then she listened to the horse's hoofs--"He has not told--he has not

43   told." That melody was blurred by the soft road. "CAN'T we have

44   the hood down?" she demanded.

Guiding Questions:

1.   Explain what Forster means by being in a muddle. What evidence does he give in this extract that Lucy is in a 'muddle'?

2.   Comment on the writer's use of symbolism, particularly in the description of the ride in the carriage

To the Reader,

I strive to make my books the best that they can be. If you have any comments or questions about this book *please* contact the author through his email: **moore.ray1@yahoo.com**

Visit my website at **http://www.raymooreauthor.com**

Also by Ray Moore:

All books are available from amazon.com and from barnesandnoble.com as paperbacks and at most online eBook retailers.

Fiction:

The Lyle Thorne Mysteries: each book features five tales from the Golden Age of Detection:

> *Investigations of The Reverend Lyle*
> *Further Investigations of The Reverend Lyle Thorne*
> *Early Investigations of Lyle Thorne*
> *Sanditon Investigations of The Reverend Lyle Thorne*

Non-fiction:- listed alphabetically by author

The ***Critical Introduction series*** is written for high school teachers and students and for college undergraduates. Each volume gives an in-depth analysis of a key text:

> *"Pride and Prejudice" by Jane Austen: A Critical Introduction*
> *"The Stranger" by Albert Camus: A Critical Introduction*
> *"The General Prologue" by Geoffrey Chaucer: A Critical Introduction*
> *"The Great Gatsby" by F. Scott Fitzgerald: A Critical Introduction*

The Text and Critical Introduction series differs from the Critical introduction series as these books contain the original medieval text together with an interlinear translation to aid the understanding of the text. The commentary allows the reader to develop a deeper understanding of the text and themes within the text.

> *"The General Prologue" by Geoffrey Chaucer: Text and Critical Introduction*
> *"The Wife of Bath's Prologue and Tale" by Geoffrey Chaucer: Text and Critical Introduction*
> *"Sir Gawain and the Green Knight": Text and Critical Introduction*

Other Study Guides available as e-books:

> *"Jane Eyre" by Charlotte Brontë: A Study Guide*
> *"Wuthering Heights" by Emily Brontë: A Study Guide*

"The Myth of Sisyphus" and "The Stranger" by Albert Camus: Two Study Guides
"Heart of Darkness" by Joseph Conrad: A Study Guide
"Great Expectations" by Charles Dickens: A Study Guide
"The Mill on the Floss" by George Eliot: A Study Guide
"Catch-22" by Joseph Heller: A Study Guide
"Nineteen Eighty-Four" by George Orwell: A Study Guide
"Selected Poems" by Sylvia Plath: A Study Guide
"Henry IV Part 2" by William Shakespeare: A Study Guide
"Julius Caesar" by William Shakespeare: A Study Guide
"Antigone" by Sophocles: A Study Guide
"Of Mice and Men" by John Steinbeck: A Study Guide
"The Pearl" by John Steinbeck: A Study Guide
"Slaughterhouse-Five" by Kurt Vonnegut: A Study Guide
'The Bridge of San Luis Rey" by Thornton Wilder: A Study Guide

Teacher resources:

Ray also publishes *many more* study guides and other resources for classroom use on the 'Teacher Pay Teachers' website:

http://www.teacherspayteachers.com/Store/Raymond-Moore

Printed in Great Britain
by Amazon.co.uk, Ltd.,
Marston Gate.